WEAL

Poems by

Philip Brady

The Ashland Poetry Press
Ashland University
Ashland, Ohio   44805

Also by Philip Brady:
Forged Correspondences

Grateful acknowledgments are made to the following journals, in
which some of these poems first appeared:
Alembic: "Lagos"
Cincinnati Poetry Collective: "Angels' Share"
Headland Center for the Arts Journal: "Siena"
Jeopardy: "Fragments of a Hammer: Work Talk While Building a
        Hotel"
The Laurel Review: "Hindu," "Silkie"
West Branch: "First Wish"

A Hebrew translation of "Priest Hole" by Ya'el Globerman was
published in *Helicon*.

Thanks are due to the New York State Foundation for a Thayer
Fellowship, to the Ohio Arts Council for three Individual Artists
Fellowships, and to the Yaddo Corporation, the Headlands Center for
the Arts, the Millay Colony for the Arts, Ragdale Foundation,
Hambidge Center for the Arts, The Virginia Center for the Creative
Arts, Hawthornden Castle (Scotland), Tyrone Guthrie Center for the
Arts (Ireland), Fundacion Valparaiso (Spain), and the Soros Center for
the Arts (Czech Republic) for residencies that helped support me while
writing these poems. Thanks to John Montague and Elizabeth Wassell
for the hospitality of Letter Cottage.

Thanks also to Youngstown State University for a Research
Professorship and Sabbatical which permitted me time to write.
Special thanks, as always, to Robert Mooney, truly the greater maker.

"Priest Hole" is for Amir Or.
"Angels' Share" is for Steve and Jeryl Oristaglio.
"Siena" is for Siena Oristaglio.
"Fragments of a Hammer..." is for Scott Strasburg.
"Monument" is for Isabelle Meglinky.
"Dawn" is for Torild Wardenaer.

Printed in the United States of America

ISBN 0-912592-43-5

Library of Congress Catalog Card Number 00-102157

For Linda

Contents

I. Hindu
Hindu/3
Creedmoor/7
Myth/10
Silkie/12
Will/14

II. Blue Baby
Dawn/23
Blue Blood/25
Blue Baby/27
A Day's Travel/28
Fragments of a Hammer: Work Talk
    While Building a Hotel/33
Angels' Share/36
Priest Hole/38
Lunday/40
Siena/45

III. Lagos
1915/51
Proof/52
Lagos/56
First Wish/66
Monument/67

I. Hindu

Hindu

I don't know how they hand out incarnations,
but somebody got shafted with this one:
to be a handsome man without much brains,
bad heart, no money or position
in America in the depths of the cold war—
might as well be celery garnish or
a goldfish a kid's plopped in a vase
on the kitchen radiator. I guess
some feckless soul in Nirvana's holding tank
thumbing Brahmin mug shots must have finked
out the wrong guy, or maybe flunked
a Rorschach test, or just tumbled, drunk,
off some cosmic platform when the character
and fate of Edward Donlon roared
into him like a train and snuffed his bliss,
and set him on a life of accidents.
Or maybe that poor soul had a plan—
for, looking back on it, you can
follow his life's pattern as easily
as a glassed-in grid map of the BMT
after the graffiti's been scrubbed off.
And even if Donlon's life force got stuffed
into the hard luck carcass of a New York dick
with slattern wife, two whelps, and a thick
skull, he always dressed with style, strutted
his beat as if he knew where he was headed—
whether to the altar or the bar,
or down to the basement to wallop Eddie Jr.
In fact, right up to the Saturday he holstered
his service revolver, climbed the stairs
and locked the bedroom door,
I doubt a single soul living on the block
thought anything was wrong—no shock
considering the cornice I grew up in—

Flushing, Queens—a post-war way station
of fenced-in postage stamp back yards,
row houses, unpithed hearts and TV dinners,
where the infirm of the hordes escaping Brooklyn
were culled on their stampede to the Island.
This was the true ground zero or ground nil
of scotch and casseroles—a lukewarm hell.
Our whole block hadn't enough prana
to incarnate an underfed amoeba.
There was Charlie Cast who b.b.'d passing cars;
Michael Stiefel, the owl-faced science nerd;
Leo Sarkissian of the pus-wet face,
Lu Anne Piazza, goosed by Jamie Wallace,
tough guy, who explained it all to us
on the front stoop after Donlon died—
(it being both sex and suicide).
He sucked his middle finger, cocked his thumb
and fired, moaning, *a-bing-a-bang-and-a-boom.*
It was just one dusk in an eternity
of fireflies and casual cruelty.
Even the Police Force looked the other way
pretending accident, so wife Joan
could get the full-dress funeral and pension.
But because Donlon lived next door and died
a wall from my bedroom, and because I wed
his daughter, Maureen, at age ten,
in a giggling ceremony in the basement
where my kid brother played best man
in his communion suit, and because
I got dubbed Ed Jr.'s godfather and because
my father's spirochettic sperm embalmed
me safely unmade till after Vietnam
and because my lover's brother hadn't yet
hanged himself, and her tumor brooded
in secret, and because no one had been
or ever would be lost, Edward Donlon's
suicide shattered some trajectory—

like the arc of the Pensy Pinky
rubber ball you imagine already homered
out of sight as you step up to the sewer
with a broomstick. Foul it off, it's gone.
We called it a Hindu—a do-over—when the sun
blinked, the physical world wobbled free
an instant, and no one saw or could agree
on what they'd seen. The moment
Donlon opened fire into his open
mouth, when his incarnation exploded
into ether, or fumes, or light, or spumes of blood—
I think I was the only one to see.
I didn't see it then, exactly,
and I was far from the only ghoul
to replay that scene in prurient detail—
the coifed, spiffy corpse sprawled on the floor,
the wife and children petrified downstairs,
and later Joan, at the wake, soused,
muttering, "I didn't think he had the guts."
And Eddie Jr. damaged as his father
saying to me, "I guess now you're my father."
No, what I saw developed slow
as a blond negative, slow
as a spectral x-ray of the splashy death,
the hum-drum life, and walleted beneath
Donlon's sharkskin suit, two secrets,
maybe the only valuables he kept,
and kept him separate from the sordid facts
he could not Hindu. The first was comic:
a rumor snaking through his drunken wake—
he wasn't a real cop: despite the gun
and badge and funeral and pension,
his fragile heart had failed the physical
and so he'd played cop as a transit mole—
a subway sleuth deployed underground to prowl
the detritus. And Donlon was not born
with a bad heart. That was the second

secret, second sight that cleaved him
from himself: a drunken night in the infinite
regression of lives before my birth that led
to his being next door, and that night led
to a car accident that killed his first
born daughter, Colleen, and nicked his heart
so that it wobbled, blinked. And this
is what I saw—Donlon wandering
the flotsamed, numbed unconscious of Flushing,
Queens, dressed to kill, searching
for the snuffed out essence my godson
was conceived in the upper world to clothe again.

Creedmoor

Between the overpass and institution wall
shadows snake across graffittied brick
and the tensile thrum of the Van Wyck
spells open their eyes. Thralled,

baboon-haired putzes thwock
handballs. Now floodlights click on
and I can name hallucinations:
Trush, Lebo, Gentile. One hundred

eighty proof. Three riffs on real.
Even a lifetime off no way I see
these three undulations coldcock every
particle of adolescent male

in Queens without a zing surging
up the spine, frazzling the ur-
layer of brain, and knifing toward
someplace where something

grotesque and unaccounted for
is about to coalesce. No diagnosis
can explain; no fist
protect. The place reason buffers,

the place you dream against.
We called it Creedmoor.
Not just asylum—a condition; a door
into borough zeitgeist

and a barb—"You're from Creedmoor, man."
We slouched against its wall. That's why
the floodlights beamed. That's why
tonight Trush flexes his skeleton

tattoo and Lebo's glare probes weakness
and Gentile, (whose name's as phony as
"Utopia" or "Fresh Meadows")
targets a knee to practice

kung fu on. Time—its pressure,
the detritus of things, the practiced lies—
you'd think they'd carbonize
old terrors, but now a cypher

squirms from the brick's maw,
face vacant as a future,
a half-demented creature—
Creedmoor, embodiment of flaw

gyrating like neon fog or a slinky
on the fritz. I've fingered three tough guys—
but now I watch the scene metastasize
searing the membrane between me

(if there's such a thing as me
in the fun-house-triple-mirror warp of rage)
and Creedmoor waving from beyond the edge
of light, screaming "mememememe"

in a nest of scabs and hair,
crazed syllables that some nights scan
as "antibodies," others as "napalm,"
sounds the world's made meaning for.

If he was only teased,
stripped, kicked and punched, spit on,
splashed with booze and stuffed into a can
that wouldn't light, it's because

the cops came in time—at least that night,
when Creedmoor drooled and babbled, failed to burn,
and I parsed myself among four primal forms—
inflicting pain, accepting it.

Myth

In the year of our lord when my lady classics prof
quieted class and flipped the light switch off,
and on the screen appeared celestial buttocks—
nymphs mounted by satyrs with huge cocks,
the scene all laced with whips and chalices,
she was maybe thirty—another species
from the tail I stalked: foxy virgins bent
on the MRS. It was sacred, she said; it meant
humans revealed as animal and spirit.
"Like a Phi Gam!" whooped a half-wit satirist.
So when she crashed the Kappa Sig keg blast
we bluffed it out. I was the classic deuch,
so it was me got shoved forward to introduce
our Dionysion curriculum.
The sorry pup I was was almost numb
from slurping grain alcohol punch from barrels.
I was twenty, bent on being intellectual,
which meant disdaining parents, smoking a briar,
and really meant transforming into the satyr
Apollo flayed for challenging his music—
the god unstrung his heart, twisted his prick,
and disemboweled him with his sacred claws.
This was a week before my father paused
from typing my thesis to have a heart attack,
a year before a brother broke his neck,
another shot, and the rest scattered
to suburban bliss. This was before
spirits scotched pud and gnawed the liver—
the divine organ Greeks thought made us human;
before Marsyas, satyr, Apollo's victim,
switched pelts with me and left me taxidermed
to bark on hind legs behind podium.
Maybe in the year of our lord of love
and my classics prof, I could have

morphed like Ariadne into tree;
if I'd translated Ovid right I'd be
a swan or mountain range or deathless spider,
instead of a trophy-mantle satyr.
Who knows? These days when I recall
my professor who said she was not beautiful
but was, who asked me to go home with her,
and I, not understanding, asked "What for?"
who spread a Greek myth picture book
before her naked body and said, "pick"—
I see my selves unrealized—
the river in that voice, the forest eyes.
The night she spirited me from the frat party
to be deflowered into mystery,
her arms engulfed, her thighs enraptured me,
she liquifacted me up into her womb,
but that ambrosia soon congealed to shame
when pals whistled, "You're one horny mother."
Then I graduated to my blood-typed father.
It was a failure to consubstantiate,
but something was conceived, and not weaned yet.
Now when I unhook paws from podium
and prowl bars, my plastered parts inflamed
to ravish nymphs, I feel her loneliness.
This was her mortal gift—to lace
fear and desire to flesh out myth.
I can't translate across that breadth.
Still, who knows? I might yet rage
and prance, hell-bent, through middle age.

Silkie

That water names as it disgorges us
is a catechism article of faith
and a cautionary tale from hit-man lure.
What separates the living from the found
is not the naming or the surfacing
but the momentary hovering over fate—
the element you can't breathe in or cling to.
Thus the breaststroke: a technique
to wave off phantoms, to clear the chuff
and afterglow of floaters that so cloy,
your goggles cake with rinds of chlorine film.
And so the rising, lapsing with each stroke
and so the laps in sonar waking dream
until the waving off becomes a sliding in,
and in a trance you find you've married water.
Because the stroke is outward, pushing away,
and because water is a body yielding,
you believe your bride is human and loves you.
She crawled from the surf and cut with a sharp shell
the seaweed cord. Yes, she was wed before
to some bull-seal, some king under the water,
but that was in another incarnation—
the only trace the salt stitched in her lips.
"Call him," you say. You want to fight
or bargain with this priapus of the deep,
blunt-headed, glistening with jism.
She mouths a skirl of bubbles and you fear
your wife's husband stole away her breath.
His glandular pupil mulls the halogen lamp;
his belly slacks along the basin tiles.
Disgorged from mother's water by the shock
of his human father's drowning, he secreted
a proofed fur and dove in after. Together,
they brood the secret of being underwater.

It galls, entrances—the thought of going down
and being whole, pure sloth and ardor
in refracted light. You feel the undertow
as your lover jackknifes down to join her kin:
the mythed, the lost, that water won't betray,
and you—but for this breaststroke, this stretching
with a frog kick from the pelvis—you'd devolve,
limn fur, arms streamed to fins. You'd follow,
moving in water cleanly, tail clenched
so not to over-stimulate the sharks.
And nights drifting to sleep there would be this:
a silkie born the day a human drowned,
and mornings when your wife peels back her cowl
you'd glimpse waves obsessed with holding on—
all the missing would lour in your veins
down to the species lost in the first flood.
They're here, swimmer, furrowing eddies beneath
your tiring limbs, ready to anoint:
Last, and *Love to Death*, and *Precious Blood*.
Every breaststroke, with a kiss, they whisper,
"Marry water, stitch your lips with thirst."

Will

after Derek Mahon's translation of François Villon

In the year 1996
right at the very dead of winter,
the mills empty and the nights dark,
I call upon Villon, clerk,
to cease his kicking against pricks,
and testify that I am he.

Although I am not poor, not locked
in slavery or debt, and though
I have no sword to hock,
the lover who despises me
joins us as one—and cleaves us too
across five bleeding centuries

with all the longing squeezed into
the human forms we love so much
we're always kneading a fresh batch
to rub together as if clay dolls
could spark. Shrugging, we crumble
them back to earth to let them cool.

Yes, I declare that I am one
with all the men that I have known—
as fatuous as it may seem
to eulogize the pimply scum
who whaled and pissed on me in school,
and number myself one with men
who've gone on to refine their skills
until a click of mouse or pen
tears flesh as well as cannonballs.

14

Still, our wobbly genitals,
staked at the V between our legs,
hoist us on a single peg—
each chafing against his enemy.
Although we try to seal our bags
of skin skin-tight, we leak
and ache and finally burst
in nacreous caves in which we drown
then shrink back, itching once again.
I am no better than the worst,
and while I would not touch, I peek
in showers and in urinals,
as passersby in Villon's France
froze, sickened, yet compelled to watch,
suspended from a wooden crotch,
hanged brothers jiggling a dance.

And more, I risk against all sense
to inch across the small abyss
created by her absence,
and, defying theorists
who hover over twisted sheets
with scalpels labeled *différance,*
declare that she and I are... no!
I can't sludge through that dreck again—
the pleas, the stunts, the promises,
the earnest hammerlock caresses.
Better to stick with you, Villon—
wrestling two into one shadow.

And remembering what I've been taught:
poems are made of things, not cant—
teacups, mitochondria, wings,
and I obey and trust that things—
our wilder, fiercer selves—whir
round and through us even now
till differences are all a blur.

But just as I insist, and drone
and sweat out this idea in verse,
the others inside me disperse,
and suddenly I'm all alone—
leaving me with nothing left
to reach across the dark but lust
(for truthfully it was not just
a finger I would thrust into
the distance dividing us).

Well, lust at least I can give back,
as Item (for this is a will)
and speaking in this borrowed voice,
I give the madness lust instills
and grips me like a palsied glove.
And if lust won't bind, then lust's
sorry lack: the conjuring from ugliness
the glow of bodies we have loved—

which is something I have done—
cruising single bars and mincing
home footless as a slinky
fumbling anonymous
body-parts, wild-eyed as sequins
to animate flesh with images—
her fingers, breasts, her gaze, her kiss—
only to wake numb and find
we are each other's succubus.

Which brings me once again to one
who pained me as she pained Villon—
to her I give my blackened tongue
in cheek laments, my bathos
and the air I smudge with noxious
words: may their mung
like Donne's hyperbolic flea
infect her memory, and perfect mine,

so that we both might see
that love is not original sin
but, like cancer cells and poems,
merely an imitation.

And to the other absences—
dead parents and aborted child,
who grasp from amniotic seas
to fill my boat with tears and bile,
to them I give the small comfort
that they, perhaps, exist in me—
as Homer and Spiro Agnew said,
the dead are the silent majority.

And for this amplitude I claim
nothing—which is all they own
of breath, of pain, delight and toil.
Yet they persist, without dimension,
but certain as flame in unmined coal.

And to this burg I'm sentenced to—
riverless, sealess, flayed of hills,
as barren as Villon's Anjé
scarabed with dead slagless mills,
this town called Young, jambarred between
excresences called Cleve and Pitt—
names eloquent as the blood-specked spit
of iron-lunged de-ghosted men—

Yes, to my adopted home
jackhammered into three cornices—
the first, a cess of rutted streets
where we frig our victims out of cars,
smoke crack, and shut our children in,
the second, deeper, where we lease
freight liquidator furniture

to slump in, bathed in cathode rays,
and last, most fearsome, the Cocytus
circle of deep cyberspace
and white-noosed, suburban desperation—
Girard, Niles, Canfield, Hubbard, Struthers—
named like a brood of bastard children,
where we refinance our mortgages,
and repossess each other's wives—

to you, Ohio, who lured me here
with lucre your laureate James Wright spurned
to cough away his sacred life
in Florence—to you I give
the fact that you are everywhere—
that nowhere where I've ever earned
what's called "a living" can I live.

And to François Villon, *mon vieux,*
reconstituted against his will
from guesswork and an attitude—
this French thief whose voice I stole,
filched once before—by Derek Mahon,
who stripped antique French to the crude
modern English left to him—
a language left in recompense,
like the changling of old fairy tales
exchanged for identity and future
French, Irish, and American—
I give the 50 cents per line
or copy and a year's subscription
prized by poets in these times
along with Vendler's benediction.

For four years on the coldest nights
(for this horror began in '92)
I've slipped out of my snoring mouth
in terror of sleep apnea,

18

regarding with a cast-cold eye
the febrile corpse I'm wedded to.

By touch and instinct I waft through
the labyrinth of my rented rooms
to key these cyphers across a blue
word-perfect screen until ennui
or a failing cadmium battery
return me to the present tense,
to my untransmogrifying I-
beam long cooled from its molten womb,
and with a spasm I release
my jism back into nightmare
leaving Villon to Parnassian fire,
and my old flame, far away somewhere,
to stir, and feel a chill, and flicker.

II. Blue Baby

Dawn

after viewing Anthony Gormley's Installation,
"Another Place" on Stravanger Beach, Norway

Fellow patrons of the first art nudie flicks,
first generation to witness explicit sex
in groups both ways in color since the Romans—
and this in the anno mirabilis '69,
women as well as men rapt, sucked in
by the plush neon bijou movie mouth
or pussy or ass—each word, each ticket punched
a gesture of political liberation—
thus Swedes, using only Copper Tone
and dialogue from Strindberg could fashion
a cult classic—*I Am Curious (Yellow)*,
and *Heat*, a domestic release, could show
male and female genitalia unpruned
not just in Nirvana and Berkeley but behind
venetian blinds of row house suburbs
and in public on weekend nights with neighbors,
nodding to Fred and Holly, Biff and Estelle
queing to enter visions of Blake's Hell
and some of us not old enough to drive.
No wonder we art loving nudie buffs could brave
Mutually Assured Destruction, consciousness
strip pokered past the final guess—
bucking in velvet, our eyes exploding X's,
we watched creation french apocolypse.
And in the seventies the need to titrate
up the level of pheromones, and yet
at the same time maintain the veneer
of art—redeeming, transformative—not Lear
exactly, but a bit at odds with weather,
led Parisian director Just Jaeckin
to subtitle *Emmanuelle* "God is coming"
and she was, and his sepia Gothic S&M

Story of O climaxed with a scream
dissolving on the tortured woman's
canines, as if in this lacquered gleam
we glimpsed the eye of the mind's hurricane,
the radiance beneath Eve's fig,
source of Kali and sheela-na-gigs.
And some of us, floating from the theatre,
hands sticky with spunk and chocolate bars
walked the earth for years clothed in
a trance lush and ineffable as the screen
images that strung our chromosomes
around the G of flesh and art, and now
I know that through the eighties when video
sex caught on and the nineties when theorists
lectured scrums of sophomores till they tssked
a few kept walking, though their bodies bloated
or drank wind, though spiders clawed
their cheeks, though they left behind for dead
all women and any man who deviated
from erect posture or expression of awe—
such was their faith they would mature
perfect they kept on all the way here
to Stravanger Beach in Norway where they stand:
a hundred bronze sculptures sunk in sand,
green with salt wind, in sea foam,
their cocks twitching at the flush horizon.

Blue Blood

in Hawthornden Castle

What's stone got to do with being born?—
flesh tunneling through flesh, quickened
by a slap. First sting betrays the plot: years
of drudge jobs, pharmaceuticals, and lovers
that end this morning, when rain fingertips
a fastness and you descend spined steps
to flagstones, and the blazened arras opens
on a glen of firs, sycamores, Scots pine,
cleft by a stream, cliffed by battlements.
Unseen hands tend the hearth's banked fire,
vermillion sherry's thimbled from decanters—
the scene's so achingly familiar
it must be you were born noble, lost and
found by rubes, smuggled down
goat paths or through sewers. But truth is
you're not Oedipus or Moses,
you're in this ancient castle for a term
in tribute to the poet William Drummond.
If you're blue-blooded it's because
you were an RH baby—transfused
into a suburb that bricks up the past,
and birth's the first chance to chisel out.
Turning to stone's a common trick. Before,
there was the yuppie antique dealer
who rooked the castle of its furniture;
the laird who stumbled off the parapet;
and a cavalier in 1338
who conquered Lord Dowglas five times
in a single day and then was prisoner ta'en—
like kids playing cowboys & indians.
And here's Drummond himself in portraiture,
Ben Jonson's host, King Charles's courtier,
well-pedigreed, yet haunted by his blood

to compose in caves the sacred solitude
graved on the stone façade to marry place,
or to rhyme over what you couldn't face
this morning, when a line stung
trembling your frail foundation,
What's love to do with being born?
But I revised to stone. I, not you.
I was afraid to ask. Afraid I knew.

Blue Baby

What's love to do with being born?—
besides the pain, adrenaline,
the thrashing up from sea,
brined with amnesia.
Then the skullscape cools, secretes
the need for touch, a secret
tongue. Slowly a soul
coagulates—so vast for all
your running off you can't be borne
from it. And what if you come
blue? What if you run so far
short the last womb's scarred?
Fear like that spawns nightmare.
Love? Machines engendered
you and now when you purr
at breast vein maps pinwheel. Brain
hiccups something to shrink from:
father; jealous husband.

A Day's Travel

It's Spain, although it could be anywhere.
Mojacar's cliffs and canyons disappear.
You duffle a fortnight's wash and zip
your bulging case. You glance around this kip—
the routine check of closet, bathroom, shelf—
it's leaving that recollects you to yourself.
In fact, you're gone already: leaving began
last night with the usual last night dream—
peering into a pool where leaves swirl
into vaguely familiar places before your internal
alarm clock scatters them at dawn.
                              An age
is the reversal of an age, said some sage—
Yeats, probably. He must have copped on
to his gyres waiting for a cab in Dublin,
though it's as hard to imagine his cream pate
withering to truth in Spanish heat
as it is to think today you'll be in Belfast—
impossible, but that's your distant target,
a spondee balanced between opposing wills
occupying the same syllables,
divided by a silent, invisible
caesura. Bad luck to think that far ahead.
Instead, you stand in a sliver of palm shade,
and squint both ways, conjuring your taxi.
And when it comes it feels like luxury
and helplessness: to rent a stranger
in a clap-trap chariot to chauffeur
seems wanton as having a girl shampoo your hair
or tipping for the best table at Luger's.
But *he* drives. You sit in the rear.
His shoulders are relentless, square as Daddy's
when you squirmed and rocked, trying not to pee.
Still you try out your school *español* chat.

Then you gaze out the window and connect red spots—
sun, reflection; absence, mountain.
Your brain splits. One lobe tenses to orgasm
spouting ghee with the multitude who fuck
around the globe today. You light up, stroke
and hug yourself, knowing yours is the only
ticket punched with this itinerary.
The other lobe shrivels to a prune
when you're dumped off at the bus station
in Vera.
          Why stick a bus stop in this dust bowl
named for a Jersey lunch counter moll?
By the time the carriage lumbers into view
flanks muraled, windows tinted blue
you're happy to fling your kit into the stow
and stoop into the flickering red nave
fearsome as the Andalusian caves
carved in dizzying heights in granite cliffs.
Squatters still inhabit them. The quiff
here's worse: petrol and 80 proof perfume
straight up. There are the blue-haired madames
and the toreadors, the creeling babies
and mascarad princesses. They ventriloquize
each empty seat with bile. All eyes
squib down. Gutted, you lurch, gulp phlegm
and squeeze past a squid-soft crenolated bosom
into a gashed rumble seat. You're all knees,
elbows and nerves. Soon your bony ass
goes numb. Your head's desiccated—
a Swedish meatball stuck on the lettuce bed
of your spent cock. You blink, bobbing
with each jolt. You become a thing.
This is what it is to be dis-
membered. The depressed underworld god Dis
erupts manic and morphs into a bus
to cruise an eternity of pueblos. He devours
and disgorges souls and gristle. His prayer

might be heaven. Yours is merely air.
At the Alicante airport the beast
hisses and slumps dead and you're released.

All airports belong to the one nation
(in Leopold Bloom's famous definition)
people living together. Or apart.
This is as close to home as you can get:
lounges, timetables, puddle-jumpers, tarmac
from Guadalajara to Mbuji-Mayi, Knock
to San Francisco. You're a citizen
of airports. Native flora? None. Not even
buckeye or olive branch. No shamrock or leek.
National bird? You don't know beak
from crissum. You'd like to be a trappist
brewing hops or a mason or biologist—
to have some truck with earth: its prodigal
rhymed and unrhymed cataloguing, its wobble,
its protozoan will, its rondure.
Inside you there are whole tribes of kearns
gathered in forests beyond range of napalm
eager to raze the skies, sharpening metal.
That's why airports are cordoned off, sterile.
To enter duty-free you must be shit-
less, irresponsible; your bones are lit
on TV, even your wit's examined
(no joking about bombs).
                          Boarding the plane
You're on the slum side of the caste system
(here it's the Brahmins who get purdahed)
so you pay for your own drinks, though you'll get fed.
Now, flight attendants semaphore
K.Y.A. goodbye, and the hull shudders
with the surge of engines sweating to engage
this hulk with air—and though the average
passenger could fly, statistics claim,
949,007 times

without a crash—your stomach torques, giddy
with the G Force of *duende*.
                              Finally
at normal cruising speed and altitude,
the bore who poked your armrest starts to nod.
You read your thriller in a pin of light
so immersed that a pair of fishnet tights
slinks by unnoticed until a jeweled belt flicks
your ear. The hull hums like a womb. That speck
you left below—your life—goes on for all
you care without you. Old quarrels heal.
You redeem every shame, from high school
piss contests to spats with deans. Old Flames,
(your lover, sneering, calls them "The Pantheon")
flicker sepia-bright before your eyes
forgiving and forgiven. You fantasize
tangles of nude limbs, nipples, coral
mouths and genitals. You're so enthralled
soon you invite rivals to plunge in.
Then your ears pop and you descend.

At the Heathrow terminal you're overcome
with desire to confess to the customs man,
to kibbitz with the Waterstone's newsgirl,
to blurt to the metal detector, "hiya, pal,"
to schmooze, palaver, flummux, belch, and whinge
simply to be yourself in your own language.

And in the air again your head lolls
between the headrest and the double
plastic port. You drowse on the corniced sea
of cloud—the sea in coma—the parabola
of your day's as hard to follow
as a curser in sunlight or stone's decay—
you might have been submerged in this antipode
of drowning an instant or decades
and when you break through the surface from above

suddenly you recall your dream of leaves
and the false serenity of Antrim drumlins
coalesces into another scene:
a postage stamp backyard, a gnarled maple
where once you spied a perching cardinal.
Yes, you might have lived somewhere. It's gone—
you won't return. What lives lives in your skin—
the blood still pulsing in a phantom limb.

Fragments of a Hammer: Work Talk While Building a Hotel

I broke against a wall of jewels.

—James Wright

I

"My hart leek blood," scrawled in
an entrance test I graded
F. But here the door's sledged
in. Picks flay walls down
to a skeleton of posts, a skein
of wires. Try entering my world:
phalanx of desks under fluorescent
light. "Why are you here?" you're asked in

code that blips across chalkboards.
No hammers, crowbars. But you guess
enough to flinch, confess
at random, "Anarchist! Sluggard!"
"That's very good," hisses a box.
"That's good. That's almost it. Next."

II

In that tense instant just before
the buzz saw blisters through the sheet
of pine that hums and vibrates
underneath my palms, as whir
rises to screech, and pressure
forces me to concentrate
on penciled line, I hesitate—
feeling the wood's grain, its scars.

Then steel ouija-es my fingers, nerves
thrill to its pull as when, taking
a tight curve in a speeding car,

or leaning almost too far
over a bridge rail, something
says jump, something in me swerves.

III

Is verse a hall of hotel rooms—
with shower, TV, double bed,
so anyone can feel at home?
Drapes, rug, wood rafters? Or is it
lightning play of mind—cold air
heart-tinted, audible to the dead—
nerve star-case unspooled everywhere,
defying sense, unblueprinted?

And anyway, why cling to form
when I can no more splice a wire
or stud shingles than I could worm
into one word, or nail fire
to a rock? The painter snarls, "Hey man—
you're talking to yourself again."

IV

First sand, then polyurethane
with even strokes. Stroke back again
into the gleam. My boss—old friend—
(who else would hire me?) explains
refinishing. Now he covers
my brush hand with his—his slim
fingers, almost familiar
as my own, impart their rhythm
and I glide with a new flourish
down the cabinet. I forget
that I've left all unfinished,
that moving is my instinct
sure as breathing, that I live
by leaving—streaky, tentative.

V

"Run down and fetch me a nipple
and a nine-inch bushing," orders
the fat plumber. "Cinch, pal,"
I yell, and hustle downstairs,
whistling. But why fudge?
My brass rings false; I'm clueless.
So I prowl the bar, giggle, nudge
the Schlitz-globe beer tap, resist...

then squint through pebbled glass into
the kitchen, where a beautiful
young girl flicks radishes. She's so
deft, sparks seem to fly from cool
vegetable flesh. I close my eyes.
Let sap in hollow darkness rise.

Angels' Share

Each spring, a millionaire from Philadelphia
invites me to spend a week with him somewhere
in Paradise. He lives there year round
but the scene's never the same: one year
Paradise is a lush island, one year a city
of nude diamonds, now it's a chateau
cradled in a cleft between two mountains
deep in France. Mornings we rise
in alabaster light; there are baguettes
and coffee marbled with cinnamon and cream;
evenings it's Calvados and Macanudos, charades
and the mathematics of post-Newtonian finance
upon which everything in Paradise depends
right down to the gold-flaked wallpaper.
High finance is so perfect, it is discussed
in virtual silence, and the more advanced
the angel, the fewer words, so when we stroll
through local apple orchards, and a peasant,
gnarled and weedy as the trees he prunes,
demonstrates at length the making
of brandy, my friend distills ten minutes
of manic French down to a few phrases:
"The apples are skinned, pulped; the cider
is refined, then casked ten years;
the dross evaporating is called angel's share."
What my friend misses isn't misery
or grimy news but the angels' share
that swirls up, vanishing,
from those of us left living with these things.
He reads my notebooks painfully, his lips
pursed like a monk's, his tanned brow
furrowing when the words don't seem quite right.
"What does shard mean," he asks, and when I tell him
shard is shaped like heart and can mean

possible or explosion, he wonders out loud
if he's lived too long where nothing's
ever broken. "Something inside me
is scooped out," he reads—it's meaningless
here where the page records the play
of light on ivied trellises or else
it means too much and he makes me reassure him
I won't die. Besides largesse, to live
in Paradise requires being paired and so
when eight bright lovers float over the lawn
and circle, holding hands under the full moon
the fact that I make nine causes a rift.
They want me to join hands with the trees,
to slice from a raw heart a shard
and boil it down and sing the vapors;
there is almost enough chill in the night air
to remember such a thing as pain, so I begin
but with all the Calvados I've drunk
they really do resemble angels, or divine
king salmon enticed from cold springs
with human song and wine, and I shiver
and barely a syllable spurts out
before the silence takes me and I see
no one is disappointed and suddenly I remember
that every year in Paradise I forget
more, and it is this that I am here for, so they
remember how it started: the slow refining down
to liquid fire, the forgetting that suffuses
Paradise with this crystal gleam, and they close
the circle, peer into my face, as if this
were their last glimpse of a world
that must, from Paradise, appear
gaunt and lightless as a wizened apple.

Priest Hole

After hours laying hands on the English
from his Hebrew in a twilit Scottish keep,
the poet reads my palm. A mass of runes—
that's all I ken of the weal I offer daily
to my mouth, but he has traveled to India
and beyond, and of dark arts, this he has chosen:
light beyond words. His own?
Branked for centuries, his poem's tongue
now quivers the far lip of consciousness
and in the timeless half-light of midsummer
I feel it coalescing, like new weather.
We are almost fully darkened with *Loch Dhu*—
black Scotch gone blind from aging in charred barrels.
This is what God must seem from a black hole.
Beyond? The poem's vanished. The last word
beckons to the darkness, "Speak."
The poet takes my hand. It opens
for the first time, like a page. "Your future
cleaves," he augurs, "here," and he kneads a wenn
forking from the pulse. "Now you choose one."
We've spent the evening sentencing
English and Hebrew to mad castling,
crabbing from opposite margins
toward a language just reborn
from God's last word, where One's
immense, omnipotent, and present tense
engulfs eternal twilight like *Loch Dhu*.
Each choice effaced the step below
until it seemed I stood on the lip
of a fell parapet, arms stretched.
Above, miasma of stars whispering
to the infinite. Below, fierce
ogham cuts; the echo
of English iron striking stone.

I take back my hand. It steeps
in a smidgeon of unearthly light.
Here is a callus called *Mound of Venus,*
horned grain whorling to the first
stroke of eternity; here *Solomon's Ring,*
skinned escutcheon figuring loss and speech;
Here *Girdle of Saturn,* aura of fury,
crowning the fate that blossoms from a fist.
O God of gnostic grammar who parses time,
I did not know your power to glean flesh.
Now I will climb down, tonsure my pate
and trace Kabballas between touch and pulse.
Only this I beg—let me keep
one venial future furled. Let one hand
dirk its pocket for a hole. Call it
the castle's Priest Hole, where hermits
mumble while hordes slaughter above
for the One Truth. O Laird, pray let
my five anchorites scribe unshriven walls.

Lunday

This is a last chance midnight A.P.B.
for my fugitive, one Robert Lunday,
last heard from four years ago in Japan
where he eloped with his ESL student
name of Yukiko, and infant, Dugan.
Last word I had was a letter saying he whored
part-time in a Kyoto K-Mart, a job procured
by his wife's tattooed Yakuza hitman father.
Last word, the scam to fence unknown
priceless paintings cut-rate had gone
under, and the stranded family was holed
up in a cold-water beachhouse and they'd sold
his father's watch to pay the bills. For me,
for anyone else I know, this would be
enough plot to distill a lifetime's stories,
but for Lunday it's just the latest and I hope
not the last scrape in a series of funky trips
that curlicue from Georgia, Soho,
Zaire, Oregon, Houston, Palo Alto—
(with a few side jaunts to parts unknown)
a wobbling arc of a friend exiled from home.
But really, there was never a home to leave.
His father, an Air Force hot-shot, died to save
his best friend on their second tour in Nam,
but some time before that the best friend
had married Lunday's mother, who then
cooked Thanksgiving dinners for both men
and a Vietnamese wife or perhaps it was
the second wife who cooked Vietnamese
and the second husband, Lunday's stepdad,
who beat my shadow brother to manhood
and left his car in the short term lot and fled
in a piper cub with some vets or drug runners
never to return. Something like that. His sister

married a biker doing time on a murder
rap and Lunday heart-brailled all this
in long, fine, savage poems, "Major Lewis"
and "Georgia Lamb,"—fingering,
syllable by syllable, the flickering
parabolas of loss. Normally
I wouldn't borrow his thunder, especially
in this country where even words are screwed
down by propriety and I could be sued.
But I can't find him without an SS number
or his mother's first name or his sister's
married name or what prison she visits.
There are seventy Robert Lundays on the internet,
so far I've tracked down thirty-seven.
I fear he's dead. It would be just like him.
This is a man who left the Peace Corps
after two weeks because he was heart sore
for a woman he'd just jilted. Needless to say,
she jilted him right back for Hari Krishna
and was last heard from dancing jigs from Sarah
Lawrence to India and so Lunday Huck Finn'd,
shagged sheep on an Adventist farm, and landed
at sea in a commercial fishing trawler
puking tuna under Pacific stars.
That's when his step-father went AWOL and Lunday
was gill-hooked back across the country.
He tried everything to find him—Private Eyes,
Fortune Tellers, even the State Police—
maybe that's next—me hounding my old friend
across unearthly borders with sirens.
Although I'm elder, it was me who followed—
you can see that in our only photo—
the burrowing shoulders of him, the seriousness
of his allegiance, not to me, but to the space
he yearned toward, his visage fibrillating through
emulsion. And me, a weedy comma,
draped over, clinging like kudzu. Hunger

beams from me. I am Ugolino's tower
gnawing other's secrets, their starved words.
Maybe I followed Lunday because my blood
kid brother Brian had circumvented
primogeniture with his panache. He wed
his college sweetheart, entered corporate
heaven—he was sealed in luck—dipped to the heels,
ever since the Beehive—the posh preschool
our parents yellow-paged so Brian, born
nine days past the Catholic school deadline,
could get a toddling start in the fast lane.
Meanwhile, Lunday and I adopted a scorched
earth policy regarding fathers—search
and destroy—then resurrect in verse—
starting with the two assigned to us—
then blow-torching the b. '27 gang—
Merwin, Ashbery, Kinnell, Wright—and Dugan,
yes, Alan Dugan, who the son's
named for. Since they were failed sons, we thought
they'd need kids too. Once, Lunday brought
home John Logan, whom he'd found wandering
bookstores like Christopher Smart in slippers begging
copies of his out-of-print masterpieces.
"Here's one," says Lunday and produces
a first edition of *The Zigzag Walk*
from his knapsack. Signed. Robert, we've sucked
that marrow dry. Watched as fathers sank,
their torsos thrashing in Parnassian muck.
I'm bald now, still childless, paunching.
My brother and I did the American thing
dropping our parents in a suburban grave
beneath one of the humming techno-hives
where Brian pit-stopped on his speedy climb
(their corpses shift in my skull's slime
like bad teeth) and I have tenure
in a valley of molten fire.
All this is absolutely normal

42

and should have been almost visible
from *la plage* of Lake Kivu in the pre-dawn mist
where we smoked *chauvre* in banana husks
and guzzled from clay gourds of *lutuku*.
Mobutu called it Zaire then, Bukavu—
since exposed and razed on network TV
as yet another prime-time atrocity—
but then, for a few instants, it whirled
around and through us, bright, ineffable.
We saw pythons, masks, strange stars—
once, we might have glimpsed gorillas
on the mountains of the moon. But they seemed less
exotic than the fact of our own breath,
which only our words and futures could confirm.
Yes, we said, babbling on while dawn
made lucid the rippling lake and mountains
beyond—refract, don't let forms reify,
don't ogle and describe, don't stay
still, for fear of shrinking the world's vastness
to a fetish and titrating the synapses
to maps. But I did stay, till the heart's blister
cooled and now I don't care anymore—
to find my friend I'll make a fetish of him.
I'll write flat out, direct—I'll even rhyme
for the lit rags we sneered at for rejecting us—
maybe some harried editor has news of you,
or some schlemeil dickering his pud
in the waiting room of the Dillard,
Georgia, impotency clinic
will read, engorge, recalling your antics.
To track you, I'll unravel my old yarns—
how I saw six falls where Mungo Park drowned—
how I tried to chisel Rwandan diamond smugglers
with Dime Savings Bank of Brooklyn rubber
to ferry me across Lake Tanganyika
and wound up dumped off in Savannah
at the mango tree where Livingstone met Stanley.

Robert, I'll find a use for poetry.
I remember the morning you set out to swim
too far, and I remember the poem
where you almost drowned, were fished out
of the lake by smirking Lubas and vowed
to try again. I hope you've landed somewhere—
even if in a tract development in Yonkers,
even if you're living like a WASP
with a nub of cancer and stock market gossip,
some Chivas and an occasional fling
with the neighbor's missus. Your yearning
might have taken you too far, too deep
to hear. I don't ask much. Only I hope
you're alive, brother, gripping a piece
of the spinning earth we once thought we'd compass.

Siena

This morning, an American girl of five
living in England wakes for the first time
in the city she was named for. Her father
worked ten years for this one week
wandering Italian fields and vineyards,
playing at being home up to his knees
in sunflowers, his shades scanning the dream
landscape his parents cursed and left. Siena
fists her eyes; her mother pads barefoot
across the room and opens shutters wide
on morning in this medieval *campo*:
walls that gave a name to burnished clay,
bricks stained darker clay from blood
of men and horses that rage this afternoon
each year in ritual war called *palio*,
pounding as if to breach the earth
that made Siena's walls. Fear
socketed each parapet with slits
and for a thousand springs Siena fixed
her eyes on the clay walls
of Valace, Montariggioni, and Firenze,
as if each town were the brow of a red skull
pounding, each spring, until clouds
withered and men rushed out knee deep
in sunflowers, each skull dreaming itself
free from names. I hold Siena's hand;
this child who lives in England presses
close in the sunlight of Italian spring;
we cross the flagstone canyon of the *campo*
and she stares at spangled *cavalieri* preening
on ornamental horses, their crow-feathered lances
tapping the clay walls. She cries. What
gallops in Siena's skull? Will her skull
one afternoon one spring be pressed

by pounding of a thousand names until
it fissures like a sun-scorched cloud?
I lean and whisper, "this is just the sky
and walls and towers telling a story," and she
cries and hugs my waist; the horses, teeth
to tail, glide round the *campo's* circle
like carousel wolves and lions, their gold
carapaced torsos fixed by lances
to the clouds. And her parents—
they tap stone eyes of wolves and lions
pouncing to life from the *Palazzo Publico;*
they turn to see Siena fist her eyes
under the stained glass of the *castellari*
where St. Catherine flayed her breasts to mingle blood
with Christ. Is the world a siege
pounding their skulls? Would towers
crumble round their knees to hear
their story? It's a story
Siena's neighbor Dante might have leaned
to hear when names pounding his skull
breached the earth beneath the city
he was exiled from. What would he say,
treading a landscape rutted with iced
skulls and burning sunflowers, to these
two lovers who fled walls
mysterious fear raises far away—
suburban parapets, billboards socketed
with pastel eyes—America—
where to lay siege or be besieged
inside the skull sometimes must seem
the only choices? I hold Siena's hand.
We watch the horses flay their riders' thighs
against the walls, each costumed horseman
racing this afternoon each spring
as if hooves could pound the dead
and living skulls into one dream: Siena
blooming, withering, and reborn

in one flashed spark. The story pounds
the flagstones but my skull won't blossom
into wound. I pass through cities
nameless, skimming earth. This afternoon,
holding Siena's hand, I turn from the *palio*
toward arched passages of burnished clay
and if my whispering could breach the earth
I'd lead her down to name anew
each cornice, and laughing,
watch them fade, so when my skull
withered to cloud Siena could
let go, rise shimmering and whisper,
"My God, what have we left? What have we left
my child, but this, our only country?"

III. Lagos

1915

The year opened with blood without respite.
In their fog helmets and breeches of worm
the army of the dead has marched all night.

As they advance, memory retreats
before the guns that telescope their pain
into years that open with blood without respite—

a barrage of sentences. A trench is hit.
The dead scream. Not all are fighting men.
Some claim they are not dead. One spits

blood, swears she never lived. The marmites
burst in the future—more of the same. In
the year that opens with blood without respite

my parents are conceived. And if they meet
then everything will be just as it seems
and I will hold position a few nights

feeling the war tremble underfoot
until I shut this history, put on
the clay uniform and set out
past years and blood, marching past respite.

Proof

Across three continents in two envelopes
I am carrying, to remind myself,
proof that human creatures,
manifest in such numbers that God sneezes,
compose the simulacra of one absence
incandescent beneath knowing so we stare
with horror and desire at ourselves.

This evidence consists of emanations
from past lives: six-hundred-forty-four
bundled articles of V-MAIL
exchanged between a GI and his bride
from nineteen-forty-two to forty-five,
each despatch stamped with censor's seal,
and opening with diminutive salutation:
"Dear Stardust," or "Dear Moonbeam," sometimes "Dearest."

I bring these letters to their furthest points
of origin and destination: Bohemia,
the very pencil mark, later erased,
where The Big Three planned to dissect Europe,
before posing, seated for Roosevelt's sake,
like a row of schoolboys—Stalin roguish,
Churchill flashing his signature V for Victory,
a voodoo of the pointer and middle finger
designed to hasten what it signified.

I lay them in three shallow holes I've dug
under a shade tree at Vitezné Námisti,
a crossroads in a village of stucco
whose name means Victory Place,
but which, to me, echoes Vietnam,
a victory here—recently erased,
dissolved into the temporal

as Lidice transliterates to My Lai:
with the twist (like the flick of the wrist
morphing Churchill's "Victory"
into bohemian "Peace") that the humans
whose destiny I share are killers.

This Place of Victory in Bohemia I found
not by addresses, masked by Army code,
nor history—writing and erasing names
into a trance of organized forgetting.
I found it tracing glyphs and curliques
of turquoise and black India ink
first pored over and passed between two forms
who have dissolved into this present act.
I am their proof: the son these letters caused,
in a future just beyond my earliest past.

Here, in letter three-hundred-seventeen
Moonbeam asks her Stardust to list towns,
villages and hamlets he had passed through.
It was October 23, a Sunday.
Sinatra's voodoo bathed the railroad flat.
Moonbeam's gaze drifted out the window
where the wind revealed Stardust in shivering leaves
and she realized she'd finally passed the point
where she could stare at a vacant Brooklyn street
without the features of her lover
taking form. Absence voodood
as leaves, as radio waves, longing so deep
its anonymous face is manifest only now
when the moon, for example, no longer signifies
spontaneous overflow of emotion
and stars don't stand for stake in the eternal.

It's only when the idiom wobbles
and the meter stretches at the seams as in
"across three continents I am carrying"

that human creatures stir and almost wake
to the absence incandescent underneath,
the way the ocean suddenly disappears
from the limbic node of the farmer as he kills
the Russian tractor's motor
that gurgled all morning through wheatfields
around Place of Victory, and he's lost—
overcome with a surge of sourceless longing
perched dizzy but alert in wheat so high,
the tires barely top the tawny waves.

That's proof, that's the first reason I sow
fetishes in three separate holes—
to let them try, impossibly, to bleed
into the shade tree's roots, which I declare
for purposes of my voodoo, earth's neurons,
forever so achingly absent,
this Place of Victory shimmers, disappears.

The second reason I pock the crux of Europe
with a penknife and two envelopes is the third
continent these letters have furrowed.
It is called memory. It is a distant
palisade stippled with barbed wire.
And on this continent the absences
whose carbon-fragile longing's buried here
squat, long past horror or desire—
a pair of torpid gods facing the sea.

And human creatures rage over this proof:
that memory resisted or erased
bleeds, bathing neurons with longing
to reconceive whatever we bury
in pliable shapes—wind and leaves and words.

This might explain the gleam in Stalin's smile
as he peers into a future his pencil's pushed

until everything but absence is erased:
Victory, Bohemia, the entire
continent of memory distilled
to names scrawled and buried so deep
in separate holes longing dissolves
into the tractor gliding like a moon,
the revolution climbing to the stars,
and not a single body to obscure
how close we absent are. How present
and alive. He leans toward us. He almost sees
the source of everything that won't be born.

Lagos

My business is circumference.
                —Emily Dickinson

My younger brother, orphaned, phones
past midnight from the West to warn
that Lagos is fatal to travelers.

These months I haven't stopped moving
and even in sleep my eyes
need a constant downward
and eastward pull.
                He reads the warning sign
in three languages at L.A.X., and says
I must not go.
                I listen
but can't follow anything that gives up
short of the far margin.
                When the doctors
finally gave up, my mother was elevated
to the top floor and I was let
sleep with her in an empty wing.

What dream makes me fear rising?

I need midnight to be spirited
over silences like sidewalk cracks
until sounds slip destination
and walking is just falling
in step.
        I could easily have gone
with my first brother: this my mother
murmurs in my dreams
in morphine tongue.

But I thought I was eldest.

These months,
booze and book gloss honeycomb
the inside of the skull.
                    Downward
and eastward, Lagos
is a hive of unknown millions guidebooks
compare unfavorably to Cocytus.
                        Sleeping
in the hospital with my mother
was closer than I've ever been
to anyone though I seldom touched her.

She didn't always know
which one I was—sometimes she thought
I wanted blood so she would turn
her head into the pillow and hold
out her left arm.
                    I was a blue
baby, transfused eight times
in my first two weeks of life.
My mother called me
distant and often joked
I was a changeling.
                    At night
in the empty wing I sang
her songs and sometimes words
channeled through me from the honeycomb
of rooms below my feet.
                    God knows.
Is that good? I'll be right back.

My brother and I crashed into each other
from opposite shores each cigarette break.

It was me stranded in California then
and I phoned in almost every breath.

My voyage is conducted by the eyes,
but memory seeps, silting up
the delta of the optic nerve. Then
words give up.
                    The doctors
gave up after the third intubation.
Intubation is a word but when remembered
it is my mother's face incarnate,
it means shut off from air and speech.

A priest translated—sometimes my mother
thought I was this priest
and turned toward me like a sunflower
toward light.
                    In Lagos
traffic and gas fumes murder sleep.
I have touched down
in a city of three languages,
all slurred.
                    If only to recall
my mother's face turning toward light
I'll translate now: trauma
means suffering if it's someone else's,
even if you once nestled in her wing.

In Lagos my eyes move downward
and eastward against dreams.
                              Movement
is a mantra.
                    Dopamine is a number
telling how tight the human network's
stretched.
                    If you've seen Lagos
traffic you know what it means
when tubes are forced down a living
throat.
          Memory seizes.

                    Sleeping
with my mother means
her death.
            If
my father's low sperm count
hadn't kept me formless until after
World War II experiments with RH factors,
I'd have choked on my own blood.
                            Death
can be hilarious.
                The last thing
she said was, *Don't cry you're getting me
all wet.* And just before that—
she whispers it each night into
my sleep-—*Where is
my first born?*
                    She liked morphine
and when she wasn't being made
to breath by machine, she said
reproachfully, *This
is what drugs should be for.*
                        Can secrets
conjoin us without flesh?

The doctors said don't worry
how horrible it looks, she probably
won't remember.
                When I
remember, the earth skids
and veers, the mind
seizes and suddenly I'm jumbled back
in intense sun under the Ujiji
mango tree where Dr. Livingstone
encountered Henry Morton Stanley.
                            Coincidence
sparks a fleeting sexual joy.
                    I travel

ear to the vanishing,
the way my brother
records his kids shilling ditties
on his answering machine.
                              Sometimes
in rage we call each other
Father in a kind of mythopoetic
Who's On First.
                    I didn't sleep with my mother
but lay awake listening to her breath
like fast spondees; she was down
to that—just breathing—and I knew
each breath was made by the fiction
of one thing following another
we call memory.
                    From Lagos, I follow
the river to the Emir's Palace near the ford
where Mungo Park drowned.
                              Can tides
quell fear?
              I returned
to the top floor and the doctor
was already there—in hospitals
they're kings—it's unbelievable
they can walk under
the weight of so much awe.

He was diffident; he'd risen
to Marin General from the Bronx
and he saw this Brooklyn mother and her son
and felt, maybe, just faintly,
that but for luck he might have been born
me.
        Me, that is, the one,
                              by miracle,
blue blooded, christened
maybe in past lives as

Mungo or Henry Morton—
                         that's the trick—to step
into that one
of a billion incarnations that won't
madden.
              The doctor said
he liked poetry
                   and for that
incarnated instant I felt human
as if my mother's body were still
free, her gaze
deepening as the jacarandas brightened
in the window—
                    there's nothing like Marin—
the hospital cafeteria is a bistro—

and I would have done anything,
anything in the world to please
him, to coax his words
into my mother's living face.
                              The Emir's
Palace has no running water, but his word
knits ninety villages together.
                                Dreams
ascend to congest the pineal gland.
                                Lagos
is a labyrinth—it swallowed
eleven billion dollars in windfall profits
from the Gulf War and it's still
famished.
              Even the desert's
breath, the harmattan,
dies in its maw.
              I returned
to the top floor from a quick smoke
and the elevator hissed open as usual.

Choosing that my mother die
instead of breathe
by machine is a memory, but dreams spasm
silent as heat lightning—I can wind up
anywhere unless my eyes
keep moving.
                    I travel to describe
an arc: an ark rocked by cloud-
exploding storm.
                    My father died
three weeks before my mother
visited California, and on days
the morphine thinned and she remembered
that he went without a word or a glance back,
she said she felt like a stranded Baucis.
                                        One night
the capital was spirited from Lagos
to the beautiful planned city of Abuja.

I found my mother naked
in intensive care, her face
wedged between gurney
and night table, her right arm spasming
like a crippled moth.

It was the first time
I ever lay down
with her. It was the first
time nothing mattered, just
live.
        Heat rises
from Lagos dirt streets past midnight.
Even at night my skin itches and burns.

In the hospital my mother talked with ghosts
using her right hand as a phone.
I learned by eavesdropping

on morphine I am not
her first.
   Livingstone missed
the true source of the Nile, but followers
carried his bier reverently to the sea.

Let the sea churn.

When the Emir entered, his peacock
miraculously unfurled, each quill
distinct, the great fan sweeping
the Aegean eyes in a design of moons.

My mother always wanted to be a wren.
She sang herself a cautionary lullaby
about a mother who murdered her baby
and was hanged.
   I sing to remember
one thing following another, but I can't
thread words.
   My mother never abandoned
her first ghost.
   He lived
with the wrong blood only
a week, and so I took
his name.
   Lying
with her in intensive care and later
with her body breathing
from memory on the top
floor, I only
wanted to unsleeve my skin.

The string
they call the lifeline is frayed blue.
Maybe I'll unfurl.
   No one

knows exactly what happened.

My mother thought she was going to see
her mother, she said her mother
loved her the way she loved me, but by then
I wasn't sure exactly who she talked to.
Seven villages claim the spot
where Mungo Park died.
                              When my elder
brother died, he left
a trace of longing deepening
in my eyes.
                    I found him
forty years too late as in
some treacly Dickens plot line
winged with harps.
                         From Lagos,
America seems heaven. For funerals,
they slaughter seven cows, but their
cows look like starved kine of Exodus.

Undertakers have an underground
air network—they drain
the blood, apotheosize clients
20,000 feet, then sink six—like
counter-clockwise Christs.
                                   Maybe I'll go.
Maybe a brother needs me. I don't know
where I'd be with my own blood.

There are days I prefer the swimming pools,
the palms, the sweet order of Abuja.

One morning I rose to the empty wing
and she was gone
and though she'd wandered
the morphine labyrinth

for weeks, I don't know
what broke free, if anything
ascended westward, or if
she looked back, but if
she did, if this was
my sweet Euridice,
there was nobody there to wave goodbye to.

First Wish

On her death bed, my mother did one thing
I never imagined: she renounced the sister
she'd cared for all her life, whispering
"It's my time, I don't care anymore,"

breaking the swollen membrane of her blood
as if in birth. It was the strongest wish
I ever heard from her. Her forehead
flushed with pleasure, her dull eyes flashed.

And since that day some days I've wanted nothing
but to strip away invisible connections
and release flesh into this moment's dying—
numb leg, skin cancer, palpitations.

And nights when I sear my gullet with liquor
and prowl strip bars with the glee of venial sin,
I long to give myself to naked strangers,
become a blind devotee of vision—

sequins and silicone breasts and bruising strobes,
ruby nails squinnying down g-strings—
let the twin fists of my brain's lobes
clot memory, flatline dopplering

and render love submissive to sensation
as in some S&M apocalypse.
But when I roll a bill and graze the skin
of the girl above my head, she whispers "thanks,"

almost blushing, modest as a daughter,
and my sight dims, something in me craves
to touch the face of the aunt I care for
now, senile, barely visible, left to live.

Monument

Now she is dead, I speak to my mother in French.
Her strokes and the strokes she nursed my father through
revealed the future: I'll die of nonsense,
my English thickening to the tongue of a shoe,

so I practice now, rerouting synapses
and teaching her dead synapses to spark,
although she spoke no French, and mine consists
of a few rote phrases that M. Laroque

(who, in our myth, was once a general
in the Haitian army) drilled into us
in high school, when it seemed impossible
to die, or care, or salve our loneliness

in any language. When she lived,
I spoke to her in scrawls, mailed from beyond
the sill of her world and so encoded
with desire they hummed mantras

as they yellowed on her freezer.
Now I'm no mystic and my grammar falters,
but here in the autumn foothills of north Georgia
I speak to the living image of my mother.

She comes to me as a Parisian sculptor,
but shaped so like my mother—
her eyes, complexion, cheekbones, hair, and gesture
I would believe she were the answer

to some prayer if I prayed or believed
any God would bother with a two card monty
miracle. I know we are all carved
from the same flesh. And we all die

once, alone. My mother takes my hand
to show her art—her sculpture in the hills—
seven pillars raised from stones strewn
on the winding path from her cabin to the sill

of the world, where she has braced a bridge
of dead limbs veering into space. How explain
such labor? Such coincidence?
Who will see the seven guardians

balanced, impossibly, like minotaur spines,
or helixes of the planet's DNA,
or tombs, fragile dolmens—
holes inversed from darkness to convey

what? My mother will not speak. The sculptor
bends to scrawl in clay, *le temps fini
disparu dans l'infini du temps.*
The stones tense at my touch; the bridge sways.

The Richard Snyder Memorial Publication Prize

This book is the third in a series honoring the memory of Richard Snyder (1925-1986), poet, fiction writer, playwright and longtime professor of English at Ashland University. Snyder served for fifteen years as English Department chair, and was co-founder (in 1969) and co-editor of the Ashland Poetry Press, an adjunct of the university. He was also co-founder of the Creative Writing major at the school, one of the first on the undergraduate level in the country. In selecting the manuscript for this book, the editors kept in mind Snyder's tenacious dedication to craftsmanship and thematic integrity.